1995 and Beyond

A Concise Prophecy of 21st Century World Events

1995 and Beyond: A Concise Prophecy of 21st Century World Events
Flaming Vision Publications
Tulsa, Oklahoma 74136
ISBN 1-886288-31-3

Reprinted in 2001, 2011. Printed in the United States
of America.

A Word from the Author

I introduced this book in January 1995 after a prophecy I received in the winter of 1994. At that time, the entire world was preoccupied with the close of one millennium and the beginning of another. Consumed with this thought, they were poised for an apocalyptic transition, dreading the judgments prophets had predicted would usher in the new century. The buzz word then was "Y2K," and most of us remember that scare. But as it happened, time changed a decade, a century, and a millennium with little more than fun-filled New Year's celebrations.

The year trudged on, and after awhile we all breathed a sigh of relief and went back to business as usual. The world did not end, world systems did not crash, and greatly feared acts of God did not happen. All was well with the world, so fears of apocalyptic retributions subsided. For sure there were incidents of terror and catastrophe, but the massive crisis that was expected to impact the world just didn't happen. The year aged as time marched on, and soon the year 2000 gave way to 2001.

It was in this climate that the words of 1995 quietly fulfilled themselves. Attention turned to family, as was predicted. Marriage was again at the forefront of society. One newspaper article actually showed one state in America imposing marriage readiness classes on its residents because they admitted that children and families with both parents made for a strong society. The advent of the internet unleashed on children a host of predators and pedophiles that sold many of them into slavery; *1995 and Beyond* foresaw this. A huge billboard in Tulsa, Oklahoma, showed a little girl exemplifying the vicious pornography assault on our children. The book's prophecy pre-reported this in 1994.

Recently, China was elected to host the Olympics, and the entire world attests to the mega mergers of mega companies. Beer companies with food companies, internet companies with entertainment companies, and so it goes. This book also revealed these events way back in 1994.

The most recent proof was the terrorist suicide pact that executed an all-out war on America, leveling the Twin Towers in New York City and gouging a gaping hole in the Pentagon. Again, *1995 and Beyond* foretold it. Open these pages and find out what else is on the horizon for our world and how it will come to pass. See how the medical field rises to the status of princedom and how the church of the Lord Jesus Christ fares in the turbulently glorious times to come.

Table of Contents

God's Word for 1995 and Beyond

The year of 1995 and those leading into the next century will see great up-heaval. Much of the spiritual loosening that happened over the last several years will break free. Many old strongholds and ancient landmarks will be torn down to make way for the new. The new wave will be the undercurrent voice as the changing of the guard, threatening for years to take place, gets into full swing. No area of the country's culture will escape its impact; and many who thought they stood solid in their jobs, lifestyles, marriages, and communities will feel the shockwaves of change as they never before imagined.

Media

The news media too will be full of shockwaves. Irresponsible journalism will cause the media to come under attack. Government intervention, although strongly resisted at first, will succeed in moving it from its princely position. Discontentment and a lack of public trust will force it to give up certain libertarian stances. Sudden shifts in political movements will stun many as the old guard struggles to retain its hold against the invading new guard. The peculiarity of the pulsing political change will be that much of what is labeled as the new is going to be largely a return to the old. Traditional values already tugging at the heart of the culture will gain a determined foothold in many spiritually starved souls. Stinging from a libertine culture, they will turn toward the home fires of the old. Much of the freestyle life will suffer during the next several years leading up to the close of this millennium as terror after terror shocks the nation into an eerie soberness.

Business

Where business is going in the next century will be on the minds of many. How they will survive and what will happen to the last generation's enterprises are key factors in the future. Business, trading, buying and selling are integral to modern civilizations. As such, there will be no appreciable loss of businesses, but personnel shrinkage will continue as consolidation gathers momentum until the majority of enterprises falls into the hands of only a few empires. Government regulation will intervene in this trend.

Small businesses will suffer the fate of the small church. Only a relative few will survive the next two worldwide economic crises. Those that do will only survive because they will be small subsidiaries of the larger empires who seek to keep the valuable concept of mom-and-pop organizations alive in the minds of consumers for profit reasons. Chains and franchises largely consisting of these will blossom from this tactic.

As a ploy to keep the image of the small business alive and the power of the vast intact, the concept of chain stores will increase. However, their autonomy and independence will diminish as empires funneling capital down to them keep a tight reign on their operations and profits. This will occur as an overflow as the unity move accelerates and affects the larger part of human institutions. Businesses, for survival sake, will merge willingly as huge companies collaborate for world market power and control. The secondary tactic for small business will come in when fear arises over the conglomerates' ominous presence and influence in society.

Unusual income-producing vehicles invented during the time will capture giant market shares by established companies. Sales, advertising, and entertainment will all achieve mammoth success over the next ten decades. Colossal mergers will take place and the much-feared monopolies will, of necessity, reappear. Electronics and communications will infiltrate every area of life until dependence upon them is so acute that the industries furnishing their services reach monopolistic proportions. There is no way to effectively stop this trend. It must be.

Television programs that involve viewers in their plots and schemes will loom on the horizon. The advents of interactive systems will make this a soon reality. Home viewers will participate in their favorite programs and input their fantasies into them to allow their imaginations to have free course. Special networks will allow viewers to tune in at will to the stories they wish to play a part in. Because of an unusual technology that will integrate their televisions with the satellite networks, they can choose their roles and fantasies. With their computer connections, for the right price, a person can be the star of his own show. The idea will catch on as egos get inflated, the public gets addicted to the "guy or gal on the street" scenes, and the talk show participant mentality is strengthened.

Together, they will spearhead a debase mindset in modern culture that fuels secret societies, closet fetishes and perversions that explode in the earth before the end of the next decade. The darkness in human minds means the spirit of ungodly erotica will seduce many into demonic sexual encounters.

A strong exhibitionist spirit will take hold and facilitate the move of this project and its fruits. Its end aim will be an interactive network hookup in every home that, at the will of the subscriber, provides free access to the private lives of citizens unrestrictedly. These hookups will serve a multipurpose, and shortly thereafter, they will become common consumer equipment for manipulation of the minds of the population. Thoughts will be projected, dreams manipulated, and imaginations stimulated until the dullness needed to bring on the mental stupor Satan needs for his end-of-the-age plans is achieved. Mind manipulation and dream induction will become popular. Tests currently being promoted to help sleep disorders will meet with success to bring about the elaborate plan that imperceptibly controls the consciousness of the culture. The strategy, once implemented, will be painless and subtle. Money will be the original underlying motive, but world control in the hands of the ordained few will be the outcome.

Economy

Shockwaves of every sort will rattle the comfort cages of the world as unheard calamity, uprisings, and conflicts take hold as never before. It will seem like the end of the world — or at least the end of the age — is at fault, but really it is not. The stage is being set for an uncanny regime that steals the hearts and pocketbooks of many nations. It will emerge on the front as a sweetheart but will turn midstream (in about three years after its appearance). It will usher in a vicious cycle of hatred, abuse, and anti-Semitism that will cripple several significant nations.

The initial strategy will be one of comfort and consolation, enlightenment and problem resolution. In the end, though, the bitter attack planned from the beginning will assault the economies of more than a few countries. The upset will cause a plummeting effect as nation after nation reels from the delusions. By the time they awake and discover the deception, it will be too late to avert the international crises that follow. Determination to resolve the monetary instability of what is deemed a pivotal nation will leave the United Nations open to cataclysmic deception. An idea presenting itself as a subtle infusion into critical but faulty economies will hide its jeopardy. The danger will be concealed by an immediate short-lived turnaround in world money markets. The success of the plan will be so overwhelming that when the truth becomes clear, its solution will be avoided because it will disable any real economic improvement. Millions of companies will suffer and jobs by the droves will be lost. Relations will become fragile between nations and they will begin to point the finger at one another to find the one to blame for their woes.

Marriage

Marriages will see an upswing over the next several years. By the end of the decade, it will seem to be on the rise. Remarriages, many of them, will occur by the thousands. A strange phenomenon will see divorced couples seeking out one another and attempting to put right what went wrong. This will bring an improvement in the overall national social conditions as the home front becomes strengthened by the fortification of the marriage institution. Children will see better parental care as a result, and couples will put the creation of a strong home life at the top of their list. On the surface, this will appear to stem the mostly youth-driven crime wave authorities have been warring against, but not for long.

Domestic violence driven underground for a long season will resurface with a fever in the new century. Laws and harsh penalties for offenders will

8

temporarily restrain the current tide of spouse and companion abuse, but other breakdowns in American fibers will inflame the emotions of panic-stricken citizens who take it out on their families. Until then, the problem will know a brief respite. The same cannot be said for child molestation. Secret fetishes will continue to instigate pedophilia and harm youth. Swifter court processes will seem to work in the beginning, but for many youngsters the next several years will be perilous. An eventual turnaround, however, will take time. Emotionally unstable parents too will take their frustrations out on their offspring, and a gruesome slaughter of youngsters again will prevail in 1995 and beyond. Serial killings will take their share of youth. A number of children will lose their lives, and others will be kidnapped and illegally imprisoned for the perverted pleasure of sexually dysfunctional men and women. Uncontrolled media license will cause this. The move will be to ship American youngsters overseas to be used in a variety of ungodly situations. It will be uncovered during the early part of next year. In the beginning its gargantuan size will not be known; but over time, the horrendous plan to kidnap and enslave children will be exposed and its leaders arrested.

Crime

Before the generation that spearheads the marriage and family movement ages appreciably, an unusual criminal element currently preparing itself to recover the souls of the nation will surface in the latter half of the twenty-first century. They will be well organized and will become stronger during the underground period they are compelled to endure by legislation. Drugs, prostitution, rioting and street crime will resurge as this new element seeks to establish itself in the mainstream of the culture. There will not only be overt criminality, but subversive tactics will also take place. Their aim will be to legitimize their existence by planting their craftiest people in the upper echelon of society. They will take control of government and politics to have a strong say in the policies and plans adopted for crime fighting. These emissaries of darkness will influence the police and underhandedly enlist those of like character into their forces. Because attention will be scattered by economic woes and funds erosion, the insidious element will succeed simply due to the overwhelming state of affairs.

Violence, after a brief hiatus, will flare up again with a boom. Jails will continue to be packed as alternative means of handling the problem will lead to drastic measures. The measures will be fought vehemently at first, but over time, fear and foreboding will provoke many opposers to yield to the almost inhumane solutions proposed to contain it.

Migration

The influx of aliens into this country will increase, even though superficial efforts will continue to try to stem the tide. Uprisings in other countries will be so deadly that at every opportunity people will seek safe haven from them anywhere they can find it. Wars, small and great, will take place in even the remotest corners. Tribal wars will be the most frequent. Countries and nations will be torn apart by civil unrest used as a diversion; for a greater takeover of control is to come not long after the turn of the century.

The Pneuma Supernatural

A shuffling of power is presently taking place in the spirit realm as principalities, in anticipation of God's next move, gear up to reassign themselves and resettle their territories along unusual lines. The number of world nations will decrease as small nations, to avoid being swallowed up, seek protection from larger ones. Therefore, the spirits of unification and reunification will explode. Combining resources and population, they will learn, is the solution to the strength of major nations' economy. America will shortly find herself having to court allies for her own preservation. These allies will for a time be faithful, but one of two most powerful nations will emerge as the strongest. Since it will be able to buy the support of any nation it chooses, the others will bow to its pressures. The control it will exercise will make it a formidable force on the international front. Here is where things will get heated. Power struggles, control, and resources will become key issues in the confrontations that come about as a result of the strongest of the nations bullying those opposing its moves and challenging its sway. Polished, meticulous, educated, and aloof will be the country who does this, but its strength and fierce military might (built underground) will be undeniable. Smaller countries not seeking its covering will be forced to submit to it anyway. Their submission will only increase the power and arrogance of the sudden power.

Small Nations' New Alliance

Asia and the other third world countries will come into unexpected accord. Out of the ordinary agreements will be entered into to protect their lands. Realizing their vulnerability due to their scattered geography, they will get caught up in the unification spirit and join forces with one another. Surprisingly, the media will publicize the most unlikely groups talking and cooperating with each other. Over the span of several years, the cooperation will turn into alliances and ultimately unions. The unions will provide the insulation and supply that little nations desperately need. Their small individual wealth will be disproportionately magnified by their unity. The idea will look attractive to other flailing countries and will catch on. This is how the number of world nations will shrink, although their populations will continue to swell. Unprecedented revenue will pour into these baby countries as investors seek to find safe places to put their finances. A few third world nations, especially the African nations, will discover buried natural resources needed for technological and medicinal purposes. Their find will inject millions into their economy as advanced countries negotiate the purchase of their raw materials. These countries' economies will be boosted once agreements are signed. They should use great caution in their negotiations because certain proposals will not profit them over the long term. They will not perceive the outcome, however, until much later.

Health

Plagues and diseases will continue to surface with new strains of viruses, whose causes and cures will escape the medical communities and spread. Reunification and unification will help its movement. Locked in the need to stay one, new nations will battle to stay the hand of death threatening large

11

numbers of their citizens. Natural disasters will further aggravate the situation as ecological upsets spew inexplicable uncleanness onto the lands. Nations' ideas to contain their part in the health crisis will meet with some success. However, the costs to maintain them eventually will become too prohibitive. Much of the economical improvement enjoyed by the strange unions and reunions of nations will be spent on combating this foe.

Volcanoes

Volcanic eruptions will become commonplace throughout the world over the next few years, even through the next century. Untold horrors will multiply as natural disasters eject fury on the earth. Unexpected and unexplained nuclear contests will increase the carnage further, perplexing and terrifying every citizen on the planet. Tidal waves of gigantic proportions will stir its natural bounds. Storms and tornadoes will become run-of-the-mill in the world as their frequency gets too numerous to mention. Natural disaster funds will erode as nations and their communities wrestle with one calamity after another. The one bright spot to come out of the world's constant reeling from tragedy is people growing closer together. They will, due to frustration and fear, turn to one another and be forced to be not only civil, but trusting as well. Families will also see a stronger knit from these events.

The American Indians

The American Indians will receive much recognition in the years to come. They will win three major court battles that will award them millions as a result. The sums of money are so staggering that many investors will arise to help them manage and use their new wealth. Their joy will be dimmed, however, by a project illegally crucified and its promised fruit aborted. Initially, things will go well; but not long after the ventures are prospering and their response plentiful, trade agreements will go sour and much money will be lost. Hostilities, because of this, will burn and rekindle old resentments. Anger and backlash will flare as the Indians fight vehemently for what is theirs. They will refuse this latest setback attempt and determine not to take it lying down.

War

An entourage of tanks and military equipment will travel from west to east for war in 1995. A painful siege will cost billions and hurt many economies. The original plan will not go as envisioned as unavoidable elements frustrate it. Victory will not be as swift as expected; many lives will be lost and nations will suffer greatly because of it. The conflict will involve severe ground fighting and an insidious tactic will add a perilous twist that sets international negotiations back for years. Dangerously sophisticated weaponry thought to be destroyed by peace agreements will hit the scene worldwide with a vengeance. Street warriors, militia, and faltering governments will all become buyers and sellers. Subterranean factories will produce them, and tracking and shutting down facilities will take strenuous effort by all world powers. Terrorism will resume with a brazen approach. Fearless agents of several radical movements committed to death pacts will carry out their wildest dreams in Europe and America. London, England, is hardest hit, but America too will suffer shocking loss. Rebels will stun the world with daring assaults, ugly kidnappings and bombings, using fire as a regular tool of destruction. Kidnap victims will suffer mutilation and murder; two prominent world figures will be among them. The trend will provoke an international dread upon the world.

Rebel success will come from a political-military genius that has infiltrated certain organizations within world government as an ally. His presence will go unnoticed because he is soothing and congenial. He is also inconspicuous and will gain entrance through comments he makes during some meetings. Eyes and ears will be suddenly open to his wisdom. His mission will be to become not so much a voice as he is a sponge. He will confide a piece of intelligence that will serve momentarily to save lives and business. His knowledge will be so critical that he will be embraced and trusted almost immediately. This person has been working underground for over twenty years and will be responsible for manipulating several world crises and terrorist events. His position of trust will last five years before he begins to execute his plan. The man is not only a genius but he is patient and his patience will pay off. No one will suspect him, so stopping him will take awhile.

China

China will bloom on the next century horizon; at first silent, becoming easily ignored. Her wealth will astound many, and she will be courted furiously for the opportunities she offers the world. World renown will come to the country through the effort of one very brilliant man who will fling the country's door wide open to business and technological communities of the world. He is sharp and has expertise in building, finance, and development. He will come up through the ranks of the military and is refined, keen, and bold. He will be unusually young when he takes control, somewhere around his mid to late forties. A successful record of achievements will win him respect, trust, and a free hand with which he will spearhead mind-boggling change. He will become formidable in his country and will be rewarded handsomely for it. This man will bring all the key forces in his country into harmony and his work will be a model for others to follow; and indeed they will. He will exude charisma, personality, strength, wit and wisdom, and will promote national tolerance of all kinds for a long season. He will cause millions to see his country through rose colored glasses and its glow indeed will be beautiful. When his season is over, crucial areas gained will revert.

Morality

The new morality touted as the answer to pleasing everyone will experience crippling blows starting in 1995. The gains enjoyed over the last decade will be progressively halted, and in crucial areas there will be some reversal. Fears over sexually transmitted diseases will make radical socio-cultural philosophies lose ground. Fearful attitudes will ignite changes. The public, of its own volition, will withdraw from risky acts, and a silent move will return society to conservatism. Teenagers, feeling the brunt of this philosophy, will slowly respond to the new standard. Witnessing the deaths of close friends and relatives will drive them to conform to traditional values.

The sobering of society also will affect the grinding halt of the fast-paced homosexual agenda in the wake of the new morality improvements seen in the marriage picture. Nevertheless, homosexuality will persist and flourish. Because of circumstances and incidents outside of its control, though, its thrust will be slowed to push it back into the shadows for a time. This will begin to be seen by mid 1995 as the wind of pubic sentiment sways the pendulum of sexual liberation backward. Nonetheless, it will flourish. Oddly, there will be more secret homosexual liaisons than when it was open, and the consequences of these liaisons will carry rippling repercussions for decades. Irresponsibility and daring acts will cause homosexuals' stands to decrease, where in previous years they would have succeeded. However, because of the inflammatory diseases terrifying the people, their former arrogant behavior will be resisted and they will lose ground momentarily.

Striking sobriety will overtake many modern cultures. Even people whose beliefs foster unlimited and unrestrained sexual liberties will fall into moderation. The onset of social, criminal, and health epidemics will traumatize them into conformance while reformation becomes the watchword for the next era. The best that will be achieved, though, is a conformance to the inevitable. Secretly, societies will still hope for cures that allow them to continue sowing to the flesh; and many of those cures will come, although others are way off in the distant future.

Cancer cures expected in the next generation will be among these. It will still be withheld. Small treatment advances with highly promising results will be ultimately disappointing. The same is true for the aids epidemic. Several new treatments appearing to ease the distress of last stage patients will show up. But marked reversals are yet afar off. Quackery in this area will increase to capitalize off the fear of sufferers, and their vulnerability will escalate. Harsh legislation will be enacted to control the merciless scams.

Medicine

In about the third decade of the next century, extraordinary medical breakthroughs will finally occur. Old diseases **lingering** for years will be wiped out. Science will advance so rapidly from the first to the third decade that scientists' new prestige will surpass any other community. Their words will be tantamount to law, and that is where heinous abuses will take place. Unprincipled members of the community will take ungodly license in areas that will horrify the public, but it will take years and no less than four political turnovers to strip them of their power. The fear tactic they will use to retain their influence will immobilize much of society until revelation of a grotesque experiment shocks it into action. They will then sleep for a while, but their retreat will be short lived.

Technology

One need not really be a prophet to predict the sweeping power that the technological world is on the verge of wielding. Electronics, ultra sonics, laser and light technology advancements will be staggering. Uncontrollable information explosions are soon to occur, aided by an unpredictable number of satellites in the atmosphere. Oddly enough, though, not all of them will be authorized. Through some scheme of piracy, the ability for mercenary groups to commandeer or build and launch satellites in the atmosphere in the next century will expand. The knowledge to do so will become so common that all kinds of regulations will be enacted to try to control the move. It will not work. The rewards will simply be too great. As the world opens to the good, so too will it open to the evil. The illegal satellite objects will be in place for years before they are suspected. When they become known, shortsighted legislation will tie the hand of government for years before it is able to tackle the problem. By then, duplicates will be made and the ones destroyed will only be dummies. Spying, warfare, and populace manipulation will be the aim of these strange lights. Privacy invasion, because of them, will become a grave concern. The finances for these illegal "plants" will come wholly from underground sources whose plans to use them to influence world markets, public sentiment, and government are presently in the making.

The Occult

The occult and ancient idolatry will become a formidable force for the church to reckon with. Over the years of its restructuring, the movement has amassed great wealth and reputation from powerful followers. Fallout from disappointment with established religion has much to do with this. Concealed developments will evidence themselves with greater strength, and then maneuvers will be behind the mien of church ecumenical movements. They will deviously exert financial and social pressures on the church to live up to its artificial brotherly love dogma and will utterly rival it in supernatural feats.

A world acclaimed and supported order of prophets will rise almost overnight. The move God began in the church to return humanity to its spiritual roots will overflow into it. The world will not be as casual or as closed minded about spirituality as the church. While the church suffers extreme infighting over the matters of the Spirit, the world will embrace them, like the Syro-Phoenician woman did who received a miracle from the highly controversial and religiously spurned Jesus. The world will see and latch onto the immense power God is about to release to condition the earth for the events of the end of man's age. Occultists just won't give Him glory for it, although their rhetoric doctrine will feature the use of His name. A false salvation conversion will permeate the theme of their message, and as the church foolishly spurns it, the world will hurry up and run with it. A government tolerated, para-psychological and paranormal move will soon take place. Because it will not permit the distinctions of one belief or faith over another, it will invade every strata of western civilization. Outright government sponsorship of certain movements shrouded in the promise of betterment for mankind will not initially expose the backing of the government. Later it will become evident; however, its cleverly concealed approval will lend an ominous sway to the ungodly pursuits of occult knowledge.

Interest in UFO's will burst forth as sightings increase. It will reflect spiritual principalities repositioning themselves for the next century. Though volumes of reports will pour in, not all of them will be false. Evidence of a real extraterrestrial presence will mount, and denying its existence will

17

become more difficult. With the awakening of people's spiritual faculties, the consciousness of the culture will open their spiritual eyes.

Many people will indeed see supernatural beings that will not be human and will not all be good. What will be seen is an inrush of the supernatural into the world; a rush of spirit beings. The press to uncover the secret mysteries of life discerned by many in and outside of the church will spark this. Technology will play right into its hands. Human and spiritual interactions are going to be common, and many bizarre, as people find twisted comfort in consorting with demons. They will knowingly and unknowingly fall into bondage to evil spirits as a result. Their doing so will place heavy spiritual pressure on the church to compete for people's souls and explain the nature of their delusion. It will be a very hard time for true Christians.

Prayer, though returned to schools and public settings, will be ineffective as disclaimers compromise and tie the hands of God worse than ever. Terror and utter chaos will instigate its return and sanction its observance in public life. A new wave of tolerance, to grow out of it, will create a place for every spiritual concept and religious thought available. Sorting them out and recovering truth will become a monumental task over the next ten years.

Deprivations caused by the reign of logic will unleash an insatiable hunger for the deeper truths of life. The answers that the lost will seek, much of the church will be unable to provide. Consequently, a voracious supernatural appetite will lead to rediscovery and popularization of ancient texts and mysticism, and along with this their heinous religious practices will grow. The gods of mysticism and mystic religions in the heavenlies will gain strength and power as many people submit to their teachers, priests, and prophets out of ignorance. Their promises of fame, world acclaim, and wealth will be a strong drawing card. Strangely, they will succeed in delivering what they promise.

Therefore, institutions to train their own class of prophets and other ministers in the supernatural will bloom overnight as they seize the wellsprings of the supernatural illegitimately. Not long after their wide scale training and education are complete, clashes between forces will begin. The established world church will find itself ill-equipped for the contest and will turn to the schools of the ungodly to learn what it originally spurned. The danger of this is obvious.

The ground root power of the supernatural will elude the church and will be overridden by the powers of darkness. Ignorance to the supernatural and abuse of the church's own prophets will see to it that its knowledge is the knowledge of darkness, and any further spiritual altercation between the two will be embarrassingly defeating to the church. Several scores of years will expire before it recovers. The monetary benefits derived from the church's deliberate abandonment of the supernatural for formalized religion will be very short lived. Once the fundamental of supernaturalism has changed hands, the church—like national Israel of old—will find herself a captive.

The Church

The Lord's church will be fraught with its own struggles. Scandals and exposés will continue. Three of them will bring down some worldwide ministries. Truly things done in the darkness will be made known. Recovery will be grueling and take some time. The reports of the three downfalls are already in the making. Still, the church's glory lining will shimmer in the midst of it all. Meanwhile, many spiritual breakthroughs will be on the horizon and a turnaround of multitudinous proportions may be expected, even though the joy will be bittersweet. Revival, restoration, and resurrection from the rubble of humanism are about to happen on the one hand. On the other hand, the years of self-indulgence and poor self-policing will have authorities taking a more scrutinizing look at the heretofore largely silent and hidden institution. Individually and collectively, churches will come under fire from many corridors of society. The church will find it must also get hold of the unification movement and join forces to regain some very precious liberties about to be taken. Indolence and cosmopolitanism have made it vulnerable to hateful legislation because its purpose, in the eyes of the world, has been obscured. Legal changes will cause quite a number of smaller churches to fold, and those who survive will do so because of mergers with larger, more stable ones.

In the beginning the moves will be unavoidable, but over time a strange ecclesiastical hierarchy will develop. On the surface, it will at first seem good. There will be strength in numbers; but before long, doctrine, observances, worship and services will be negatively affected. They will all become rigidly regulated from within, with control of the church by the third decade of the next century being in the hands of a few unscrupulous ministers. The event will take place so stealthily that the wider part of the body will be asleep through it all. Meetings are currently being held in secret circles around the globe to position the body of Christ for religion, as they call it. For this very thing, propaganda will be printed and doctrine altered to accomplish this pseudo ecumenical movement.

The unity movement will, at the outset, empower the church so that its sheer size halts the flood of godless persecuting legislation scheduled to come down on it. Government movements inspiring them will be five years in the making. When they are in effect, though, the united church will rise to overturn volumes of laws enacted against its health and autonomy. Its actions will bring a strange fear upon society, but the church will experience horrendous backlash from within because of it.

While the bulk of the attention is put on the legal restoration movement, those plotting to control the consciousness of society through religion will have made extensive headway. They will have gathered the trust of the masses and attracted a following of immeasurable proportions. The idea of there being one world church will have taken hold, and the next move the body engages in will be the permanent solidifying of the pseudo church to rival the kingdom of the Lord Jesus Christ. Outright force will not be the method of seduction and coercion, but charismatic appeal and life compatible religion will seduce the congregations into acceptance. World changes mentioned earlier will cause Christians to turn their attentions to life under the sun. They will be preoccupied with family, finances, world events and crises. Subsequently, they will leave the subject of their spiritual life in the hands of those who are plotting to be in charge. New and irreligious ideas will be voted on and resolved before the better part of the body learns of them.

Before they know it, what was agreed upon in private sessions will have become law — at least for the church.

To handle the problems associated with diversity of faith, artificial religious movements will commence that have little to do with God or Christ. They will be mainly social in emphases and will focus on the appetites of the membership. Cycles of these moves will dominate the church during the latter half of the next century. Dogma, doctrine, faith, and practice will all be unified into one theme that encourages all to pursue their own course to God. The messages will be eloquent and highly public speakers will be hired to propagate and popularize them. Eyes will be on the images of the most appealing of personalities used to spread the word and unify the following. Those who dissent will find themselves in severe battles that include lawsuits, courts, and jail stints.

There will be little understanding of the truth, for the most part, over the next decade, as these religious merchants will have done their job well. The issue will be a matter of perspective, and followers will be goaded into seeing and interpreting religion and the Lord as they envision them. Imaging and conceptualizing will be big in the years to come. Their popularity will unleash vile rule of vain imaginations as in the days of old. The church will pick up on this mania and adopt its principles, which will be used to seduce it even further into carnality. Its delusion will enslave it to austere unrighteous leadership that will have a hold on its mind and soul.

God and Christ

God and Christ will not be silent during these events, but to the church they will seem to be. Firm and authoritative leaders will rise up alongside others from the groups who refuse the false unity move. These will protest the antichrist's agents and will suffer greatly for doing so. Their reach and audience will be drastically smaller than the organized church's, but extreme supernatural backing from God will allow their voices to be heard. These messengers will convince the masses in many unseen yet tangible ways. The antagonism they generate from the pseudo order will cause accusations of fostering schism in the body. Nevertheless, their

21

ministries will exert tremendous power on the counter-religious regime. They will be persecuted viciously, though they will also be victorious.

God will manifest Himself to His church again blatantly. It will start in small circles, and outbreaks of **fiery** evangelism will again consume the planet. His word in truth will go forth in a flurry of activity to cement it in the minds and subconsciousness of the culture. The year will see the beginning of a new demand upon established ministers and their ministries. Up and coming ministers will replace many currently esteemed messengers. Those who have been groomed in the wilderness of alienation and rejection will be awakened with startling visions and dreams. Several of these will experience supernatural encounters with the risen Lord, and will be personally instructed by Him for their work. Vast impartations of knowledge will be poured into the church, largely through what these messengers bring to the kingdom's service.

Reorganization after reorganization will occur as the present leadership is displaced. Candles will be removed from their heavenly lampstands as ministers who have ignored God for decades see thousands of followers diverted to the agents of the new move. The switch will happen so quickly that suddenly people will hear members asking, "What ever became of so-and-so?" Truly the power the world is waiting for will explode in the church. After the novelty has worn off and the price of allegiance is to be paid, though, numerous disciples of Jesus Christ will apostatize. They will do so inwardly so external evidence will not appear for years. Yet in times of significant decision making, they will secretly vote against the agenda and move of the Lord. This is how the events described above will take place.

Elijah's fire, Paul's power, Peter's brashness, and Moses' authority will resume in the church in 1995. Initially, calls for their anointing will go out far and wide. After their spirits have been reestablished in their modern day counterparts, discontentment and rebellion will come.

Aaron will falter and Korah will rise up. Mount Carmel will repeat itself again and again, and clashes with the false will become so spectacular that they make the news media. They will no longer, under these circumstances, be able to ignore what is happening in the sphere of the church's earthly life. Tabloids will report them for gain, and this will cause some true ministers to back down. That will be a grave mistake. Others will pursue and prevail.

The great exploits spoken of by Daniel the prophet and by those who know God are just around the corner. The church's next few years will be glorious, and forgetting them will be next to impossible. Conversions, spontaneous deliverance, church enrollments and returns to the Christian faith will flood the body from January 1995 onward. Testimony after testimony will talk about the miracles and power demonstrations the Holy Spirit pours out. This period will seem much like a return to the infancy days of the church.

Schools started during the next five years will be successful, and many will become the new era's flagship institutions. The hunger spoken of earlier will first be sought in or through the church. Only a few founders, however, will see that what they deliver meets the future needs and challenges of the body. This will be unfortunate. Those who do will know explosive success. They will see enrollments of untold proportions. Funds will miraculously appear as God seeks to get the revelations He is currently unfolding out to His body fast. Older institutions who refuse to progress will close down.

The year 2000 will record the demise of many heretofore prominent Christian schools. They will blame it on lack of money and support, but fear and stubbornness are the real cause. Out of their fall, however, the new schools will grow. There will be slight cooperation between the two, but the polity of the older schools will preclude them from making much needed changes. It will cost them ultimately.

God's favor will be on many persecuted as David was, beginning the first day of 1995. Those who have been underground will be heard with a new attention. The veil of the old that had blocked the listeners' ears will be lifted, and those who hear in the next few years will hear with new ears. Calendars presently filled with ineffective servants of God will be changed. Startling cancellations will be experienced that will cost thousands of dollars. God will shut many customary doors in order to open them for the move He has just actuated. Mainly, He will do so because numerous present move ministers have changed His message and capped His Spirit.

Therefore, significant and profitable ministry dates for the liberated Davidic ministers will start almost immediately after January 1, 1995. The names of pruned, promising ministers called aloud in the spirit will be heard by established Christian institutions, and they will be summoned to bring the new word and move God has talked about in the spirits of hungry leaders.

Power and authority will change hands as the astute leaders discern the times and seasons to recognize those sent to them or set in their midst. Those who do not discern will see the downside of the next move of God and will likely be a victim of it. As the book of Revelation chapters two and three echo repeatedly, "He that hath an ear, let him hear what the Spirit saith unto the churches."

About Dr. Paula Price

Paula A. Price is a strong and widely acknowledged international voice on the subject of apostolic and prophetic ministry. She is recognized as a modern-day apostle with a potent prophetic anointing. Active in full-time ministry since 1985, she has founded and established three churches, an apostolic and prophetic Bible institute, a publication company, consulting firm, and global collaborative network linking apostles and prophets together for the purpose of kingdom vision and ventures. Through this international ministry, she has transformed the lives of many through her wisdom and revelation of God's kingdom.

As a former sales and marketing executive, Dr. Price effectively blends ministerial and entrepreneurial applications in her ministry to enrich and empower a diverse audience with the skills and abilities to take kingdoms for the Lord Jesus Christ. A lecturer, teacher, curriculum developer and business trainer, Dr. Price globally consults Christian businesses, churches, schools and assemblies. Over a twenty-year period, Dr. Price has developed a superior curriculum to train Christian ministers and professionals, particularly the apostle and the prophet. Her programs often are used in both secular and non-secular environments worldwide. Although she has written over 25 books, manuals, and other course material on the apostolic and prophetic, she is most recognized for her unique 1,600-term *Prophet's Dictionary*, and her concise prophetic training manual entitled *The Prophet's Handbook*. Other releases include *The ABC's of Apostleship*, a practical guide to the fundamentals of modern apostleship; *Divine Order for Spiritual Dominance*, a five-fold ministry tool; *Eternity's Generals*, an explanation of today's apostle; and *When God Goes Silent: Living Life Without God's Voice*.

Her ministry goal is to make Christ's teachings and churches relevant for today. "Eternity in the Now" is the credo through which she accomplishes it.

In addition to her vast experience, Dr. Price has a D.Min. and a Ph.D. in Religious Education from Word of Truth Seminary in Alabama. She is also a wife, mother of three daughters, and the grandmother of two. She presently pastors New Creation Worship Assembly in Broken Arrow, OK.

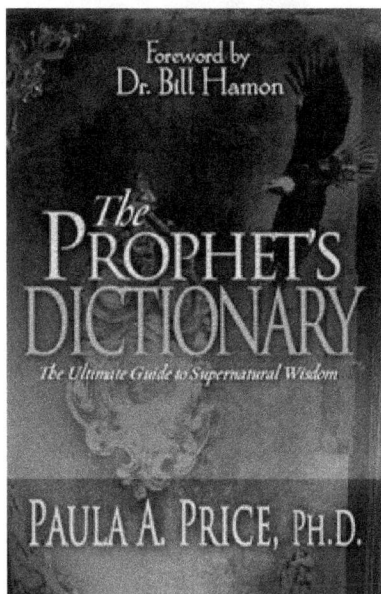

THE PROPHET'S DICTIONARY

The Ultimate Guide to Supernatural Wisdom

The Prophet's Dictionary by Paula Price is an essential tool for laymen, prophets, prophesiers, pastors, intercessors, and dreamers of dreams. As an all-in-one dictionary and reference book containing over 1,600 relevant definitions of terms and phrases for the prophetic realm of Christian ministry, it exposes ancient religious seductions and how they have infiltrated movies, television, and books. Prophetic visions and clues to interpreting their symbolism, imagery, and signs are also included. *Now available in Spanish!*

$25.95

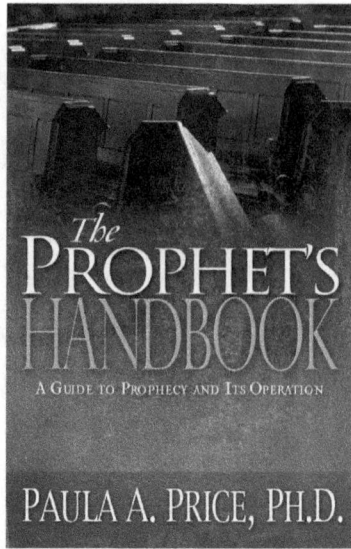

THE PROPHET'S HANDBOOK

A Guide to Prophecy and Its Operation

The Prophet's Handbook: A Guide to Prophecy and Its Operation by Dr. Paula
A. Price is a companion text to the acclaimed, *The Prophet's Dictionary:
The Ultimate Guide to Supernatural Wisdom. The Prophet's Handbook* details
the roles and duties of the prophetic in the church and clearly explains
its necessity. As an indispensable reference, this comprehensive text is
something no church leader should be without. Dr. Paula Price
intelligently and skillfully explains the function and responsibilities of
local church prophets and those who prophesy. Her years of research
and ministry have led to the ultimate guide to prophecy in the local
church.

$16.99

Introducing the Standardized Ministry Assessment Series
How do I test my Spiritual IQ?

Use our standardized ministry assessments to help determine where you fit—whether in ministry or business; find out how equipped you are for your calling, and evaluate your readiness. Our assessments are essential tools for Christian ministry that aid in assessing the potential and proficiency of those claiming or exhibiting ministerial aptitude or giftings in action.

Purpose for Destiny (PFD)

Have you ever asked yourself, "*What was God thinking when He made me*?" Are you a leader with members who seem like square pegs in round holes? If so, the **Purpose for Destiny Questionnaire** is ideal for you or your team.

Ministry Assessment Questionnaire (MAQ)

The MAQ is for any minister, leader, or gifted individual called to serve. It is an assessment created to identify the various features of five-fold ministry at work in an individual, as exhibited and/or practiced by the ministries featured in Ephesians 4:11 and I Corinthians 12:28-29.

Prophetic Aptitude Questionnaire (PAQ)

For prophets, intercessors, psalmists, seers, prayer warriors, and the like, the PAQ is an evaluative assessment tool to help Christian leaders evaluate those entrusted to their prophetic oversight or tutelage and to determine where their prophetic ministers may best serve. The PAQ is ideal for individuals interested in understanding their prophetic identity.

Apostolic Diagnostic Questionnaire (ADQ)

The ADQ is for apostles—seasoned and new; prophets—new and veteran; and pastors and church leaders inclined to apostolic ministry. It pinpoints whether you are called to serve officially in apostolic ministry or operate in the gifting. The AAQ reveals your strengths, weaknesses, and areas that need training and development.

What is the value of these assessments?

- Connect ministers with identity and calling
- Join leaders with a profitable tool for ministry selection
- Unite students with guidance and direction
- Link readiness programs with accurate evaluation of their trainees

For more information, visit www.drpaulaprice.com or call (877) 649-7764 to speak with an assessment representative.